A MELODY OF WORDS

Other books by the Author:

A Quiet Voice
A Parasol of Leaves

ANTONIA B. LAIRD

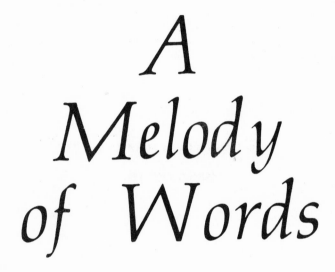

A
Melody
of Words

THE GOLDEN QUILL PRESS
Publishers

Francestown   New Hampshire

Library of Congress Catalog Card Number 78-68402

ISBN 0-8233-0286-5

Printed in the United States of America

To Walter J. Laird, Jr.
"Forever isn't long enough"

ACKNOWLEDGMENTS

Grateful acknowledgment is made to the following, in which some of the poems included in this book were first published: *Ladies Home Journal, Wilmington Morning News, Garden Club of America Bulletin, Stowe Reporter, Delaware Today, Encore* and *Major Poets.*

CONTENTS

A MELODY OF WORDS

GOOSE POND

One paddle cuts through silence
in its upward curve,
draws it down
beneath the water
in a single sweep.
Goose pond wears feathers
made of wind,
wide wings of calm,
and underneath its belly
trout play hide and seek.
Anticipation is a line, a fly,
a swirl, perhaps a fish.
If not, there's time
for one last cast
before night nibbles at the trees,
and geese fold up their wings
and go to sleep.

WIND

Wind,
his wide cloak
lined with a black cloud,
a braid of darkness
tied around his waist,
pressed thumbs
against my eyes.
Long slender fingers flattened
down my hair
until it streamed behind,
a banner to his name,
while from his velvet sleeves
the raindrops scattered
on my head.
I shrink in size
before the power
in those hands.
White-shirted giants walk the sea,
stout trees bend down
before the presence that is
wind.

A CHILD'S BALLOON

Escape,
untwine your slender tail
from tiny fingers,
hoist your chubby shape
into the air.
Sail far,
your green, red, orange dress
a harlequin of color
in a pastel sky.
Reach up and let your stomach lie
against the clouds,
drift down where heat waves garbed in sun
will carry you on shoulders
made of wind.
Explore
this world of lazy flight
until the lights of evening
touch your tail,
then fat balloon
grow thin,
and I will anchor you to earth
with magic string.

HEAT

I have stepped into a Van Gogh painting.
Heat has exploded my mind.
I have swirled my thoughts
in brown and gold,
trapped them in a field of sun,
walked through trees
that have no shade,
stretched my arms
to find a sleeve of green,
to have it turn to flame
beneath my feet.
Blue shimmers in an empty sky.
Hot sun stabs my eyelids,
burns my brain.
I stand as captive
bound with veins of heat.

TO THE LOCH NESS MONSTER

Don't let them find you.
They'd put your face on film,
freeze dry your soul in celluloid.
Those lazy swims on summer days
would all be gone.
They'd build a pen of steel,
hand feed you when
the clock strikes twelve.
You'd hate the clapping —
humans make a lot of senseless noise.
My dragon, you have lost your knight.
You've slept the centuries away.
While you rested in your loch
your prehistoric sea
grew feet of clay.
Please burrow deeper in the silt,
hide your grin behind the dark,
so children forty years from now can say,
"a man in Scotland saw the Loch Ness monster
surface yesterday."

COSTUME PARTY

I don't usually like costume parties.
I went to one dressed
as a black cat.
My long tail got in the way
when I danced.
I washed off my whiskers before dinner.
My dinner partner, a Boccaccio monk,
stroked my leg during the toasts
and told me he loved me.
I had not seen him before
nor would I see him again.
His robes got in the way when we danced,
but for a fat man he had quick feet.
I don't like to talk to people
who wear dark glasses.
Glasses hide eyes.
At the party people hid their eyes
behind masks, fans and rubber faces.
One man wrapped his face in bandages,
I don't know why, perhaps he was a fool.
It was a waggish night.
I love to dance, drink wine and talk
to people behind their eyes.
It was hard to hear in my black hat.
My long tail got in the way when I danced.
But a monk told me he loved me.
He had quick feet.

SUMMER 1977

I have watched this summer
arch its back,
reach out its claws to catch the sun,
lick off the warm fresh rain
with lazy tongue.

I have heard this summer
stretch its wings,
lift up its beak to spear the wind,
swoop down across the lake
in restless flight.

I have seen this summer
disappear
on paws of gold and brilliant red.
Between the jaws of autumn,
summer's dead.

MIDDLESCENCE
(The age between forty and fifty)

It must be middlescence,
I am angry without cause.
Emotions range from boredom to despair.
The wisdom I was given
has been turned the wrong side round,
I'm walking up a downward moving stair.

How will I be at fifty?
Will a sudden golden age
come carry off this middlescent gloom?
A renaissance of laughter,
a galaxy of smiles,
emerging from the dark side of the moon?

THE BRIDGE LESSON

Four minds,
each encased in its shell
of nerves and bone,
learn bridge
from Helen, lady of the cards.
Her brain is edged in spades
with a ridge of trump,
but her smile is an overtrick,
the balm to be rubbed
in a shredded mind.
We follow her lead
through fields of bidding,
past wild thickets of lies,
under hedges of misinformation,
to reach the fishing streams
where the slamming current runs
too fast for our lines.
Years later we arrive breathless
on the north-south side of the bridge table,
to play as Helen plays
and win the prize.

A MAN FOR ALL SEASONS

Will you walk with me
when leaves are budding on the trees,
before the ripening of fruit,
to see if love this year
will wear a spring-brushed suit?

Will you smile with me
beneath a summer sun,
your blue eyes washed in golden light,
still wrap your arms around me
on a humid night?

Will you share with me
the rotund pumpkin's smile,
cold mornings when the wild geese call?
Are you a lover who has saved
his best for fall?

Will you stay with me
when cold has crossed our palms with frost,
the wood is gone, the fire low?
I'll keep you warm
when winter winds are gusting snow.

THE COMMON COLD

A red-nosed ferret
in a cocoon of blankets,
growling words
only a fool would try to understand.
Wishing he were dead
and underground,
instead of bedded down
with a cold.
Surrounded by his lozenges
and syrups,
colored capsules,
glasses filled with juice,
he is a potentate
of misery
no one wants to see.
He rules a kingdom
where it's hard to breathe,
between the siege of sneezes
and the volleyed coughs.
Time floats through the bedroom door.
Will my red-nosed ferret
ever be a handsome Prince?

FOREVER

Forever
is a long time,
but it gets shorter
when you're over forty.
I want to live
in this house with you
forever.
I love the woods
as a backdrop
for the geese,
the brambled fields
as cover
for the Ring-Tailed Pheasant
and his bride,
the rabbit restaurant
of weeds and clover.
All share with me
until forever's
over.

BORES

They have round thoughts,
all edges smoothed,
no grooves to trip unwary
ones who pass.
Snug harbors
ringed with words that soothe.
A pack of kennel dogs
who never chase the fox.

They live small lives,
their voices never catch the sun
but speak in circles
in a dull gray square.
In houses that are dead with age
their minds are full of keys
that turn no locks.

A QUICK THOUGHT AFTER A LONG MEETING

The egotistical man often
takes a long time to say nothing,
using a lot of descriptive adjectives
and passive verbs,
as though the sound of his own voice
had begun to enchant him,
a Minotaur in a labyrinth of words.

The simple man in his unassuming and guileless way,
speaks seldom and slowly,
having no pretentious desire to roll vowels and consonants
across his tongue.
He reaches the end of the maze
surprised to find he's still holding the string.

The perfect Chairman seizes the string,
wraps it artfully in a ball,
slays the Minotaur,
while composing the victory arietta
to be sung.

LOVE'S SPELL

Love is witchcraft
when you hold my hand,
and promise music
we alone can hear.

A melody
of words and touch,
you're whispering magic
in my ear.

GLASS EXECUTIONER

Your shoulder
killed the bird in flight.
Flung from his pinnacle of air,
he soared beyond the echo
of his wings and died.
Did he expect to find a tree
high above the bowl of fall-tipped leaves,
to preen before a looking glass
with gilded trim?
Or did he hear another Gold-Crowned Kinglet
call his name?

NEVER UNDERESTIMATE

You have a scientific mind.
You don't believe in wizards,
witchcraft or a gypsy's curse.
You ride a horse
that left his wings behind.
You'll never hear a mermaid sing
or find a dragon's scale beneath a tree.
I hear your wisdom laughing down at me.

I'll find a scale of emerald green.
I'll charm the gypsies,
plait a loveknot in my hair,
drink strange potions,
read my fortune in the cards,
until I find
I've trapped my love,
despite his scientific mind.

LOST ILLUSIONS

It's summer,
winter bellies are exposed,
bathing suits reveal
the waffled thigh,
albino elephants go waddling by.

It's summer,
flesh is turning on the spit,
glistening in oil,
rare to well-done,
alligators basking in the sun.

It's summer,
there are no secrets left to guess,
illusions lie in pieces
by the pool —
until September dresses up the fool.

A SUMMER SWIM

I remember stepping in the pond,
black mud curled between my toes,
weeds tickled at my thighs and clung,
a water snake brushed lightly by my arm.
The branches of the willow hung so low
that I could hardly see you smile
and whisper, "all the turtles are asleep."

Invite me now to step into your pond,
to swim amidst the clinging weeds and slime.
I will do it on a dare,
if you will trap me thirty years of time
and hide it by the turtles' snare.

ENGLISH WAR POETS

Your poets marching through the war,
beneath the cannon and the gun,
knee deep in mud, death's shadow
pinned behind each tree,
write not of England's soil and rain,
of heather brushed with purple light,
of honor and the final great parade.

Their poems smell of blood and pain,
of brilliant men with shattered brain,
of coward next to hero in a trench.
Yet when the bones are swept aside,
those Englishmen on foreign soil
perhaps have gentle thoughts
of heather in the rain.

RIKKI-TIKKI-TAVI

A wistful thought,
a chance remark,
brings back a memory —
I had a child's blithe heart.
You read me Kipling after dinner
when the day grew dark.

A bungalow, a garden,
two cobras lay in wait.
Nag inside the bathroom,
Nagina near the gate.
Darzee called a warning,
Rikki-Tikki jumped in time,
that was the beginning
of the cobras twisted crime.
Your voice held such excitement,
I could see each clever trick.
Rikki smashed the cobra's eggs,
Rikki-Tikki-Tikki-tick.

Now dark is night
and warm is cold,
you have died and I grow slowly old.
But up in heaven, so I have been told,
there lives a red-eyed mongoose,
brave and very bold.

SNOWDROPS

My friends look old
by January light,
the grays of nature
grafted to their skin.
Their eyes expressionless,
devoid of light,
as though the cold of winter
sulks within.
All laughter cut by blades
of wind and ice,
depression hangs like crystals
in the air,
until one morning
clumps of snowdrops bloom,
in flower beds
that had been starkly bare.

CATERPILLAR

Lie down
in the winter sun.
Speak to no one.
Dream away the hours
and the days.
Spin a fresh cocoon,
let old cells die.

Rest inside
a dried, spun place.
Wish for no one.
Shapes and sinews
meet with a deep sigh.
Soft as your new wings,
let silence lie.

Butterfly,
from your warm sleep
wait for no one.
Spread your wings
in worship to the sun.
Flight and fantasy
are born as one.

ONE MORE DANCE

I hold still the essence of my youth,
I love to dance until the breath of dawn.
Throw silver slippers underneath a tree,
in evening dress race barefoot on the lawn.

My heart, my soul, my legs were made to dance,
champagne and I will never disagree.
What good all this if every man I like
leaves parties now at twelve instead of three?

LAKE LADY

Last night a regal lady,
calm and cool,
diamond studded combs
behind each perfect ear,
reached up to gently lay
her cheek to mine.

This morning she's a bitch,
rough-tongued and coarse,
her sequinned dress too gaudy
for the noonday sun.
She slaps my face
before she turns to run.

SPOONS

Why in books do lovers sleep like spoons,
as though one life could curl so close
against another,
sleep without the turning of a leg,
the cramping of an arm?
No spoon would have your neck,
your ears to tickle with the warmth of breath,
your shoulders waiting to be hugged,
until you turn to catch the lips
that linger on your back,
thrust all thoughts of sleep
into a drawer with silver spoons.

THOUGHTS ON A CHAIRLIFT

I have spent days
in idle conversation,
for a week have harvested nothing.
I have listened to a treatise
on boots, skis, trail conditions
and weather forecasts.
I have listened again.
Trapped by this winter storm of words
I have built an igloo
with a smile in front.
Behind the ice
I recite poetry,
plan imaginary trips,
and talk to men who have
warm hands, bare feet,
and summer in their hearts.

A CURSE

Come spectate — be my guest
and watch.
Come step inside my heart
and hear it beat.
A voice is babbling,
could the fool be me?
I've never begged for life before.
Repeat — repeat,
it's ten of nine,
it's ten of nine,
I have no cause to lie
to you, black man.
What difference is the time
if I am dead.
Your words and gun
won't tie my feet.
I'd rather die
than be a wildman's feast.
Still running free,
I hope my money turns to powder
in your hands
and blows your brains to hell.

SOMEONE TO LISTEN

Sometimes there are moments we must listen,
hear the sparrow's wings fold slowly down.
Over us an endless sea of prattle,
tangled up and trampled to the ground.

Sentences grow backward in confusion,
flying through the dusk to find the night.
Waiting for the words to have an ending,
as birds who circle long before they light.

If the day has ceased to hold a meaning,
and falls between the stepping stones to drown,
then talk and I'll be there to listen,
in case an eagle's wing comes floating down.

YOUR CHOICE

If you don't want me,
tell me now.
I will travel just as far
as ships will sail,
and all the mermaids in the sea
will listen to me play
my gold guitar.

If I am just a bother,
don't explain.
I'll read the message in your eyes,
and I will fly
to distant lands,
write the poetry of you
in foreign sands.

If I now bore you,
love has gone.
So I will board
the fastest train,
and when the nights are edged with ice,
I'll hear the whistle
call your name.

But if you shout in anger,
I will stay.
For sparks will change to fire
as the night to day,
I'll have another glass of wine,
and think of words
of love to say.

HOUSEGUESTS

Let them play tennis, golf, croquet,
at waterskiing quite excel,
but unless they like to read,
a rainy day with guests is hell.

JOHN McCOY'S PAINTING, "TREES"

Out of the mist now dense, now sheer,
fir trees fade, then reappear.
Shadows form, then slip away,
night ascends the scale to day.

Full clouds swirl, soar, sail and twist,
blue to gray and gray to mist.
Paint holds lightning by the sash,
listen, hear the raindrops splash.

SEE-SAW

Your even disposition
must be dull.
No troughs or peaks,
no moments of despair,
no wish for something,
someone who will never be.
You walk an even line
between the driest desert
and the deepest sea.

Today I'm in a dungeon
filled with gloom,
tomorrow on a mountain
bathed in sun.
I either beat the Romans
or the lion has a feast.
You smile, I only laugh or cry.
A see-saw throws me down
or lifts me high.

MOVING

I will go and sit
alone in my empty house.
I will have no lights,
no doorbell, no telephone.
I will ring myself in silence,
sit alone in my empty house.
Think strange lonely thoughts,
dream deep lonely dreams
though I'm awake.
The doors will hide
my sudden flight,
the windows wrap my solitude
in sun.
Trees on a distant hill,
birds in the air
will keep my secret
from a chill March wind.
Too soon the rooms
will fill with life,
the doorbell chime,
the phone will ring.
I'll never be alone
in my empty house
once it is spring.

BLIND

Reach out and touch my hand
so I can reassure myself
that it is you.
In one short month
my day has just become a synonym for night.
Dark shapes stand firm,
grey blends to grey,
what is the proper answer
when they say
you're blind?
Pity, rage, acceptance
race each other through the stretch,
hope lies tangled in the field,
and I must follow
with a shuffling gait
behind.
One year or three,
what will I do with life
or life with me?

CAMEL'S HUMP

Out of the clouds he humps his back,
rests his snout on a windy stair.
Tied to the earth by roots of stone,
his round head ruffles the freezing air.

Snow lies thick on his shoulder blades,
icicles sprout from both ears.
He belongs to a winter world,
proud in a vest of crystal tears.

MADNESS

In the asylum
inmates are writing poetry.
Thought therapy,
word tonics for a frozen mind.
Underneath the verbs
ice daggers stab at participles
on a twisted line.
Long johns dark with age
flap out each sentence
for the therapist to catch.
Round square,
hatch out a poem
you can show and tell.

A.E.B.

The day you died
the sky turned just the color
of your eyes
to say good-by.
Your wisdom and your love
have passed beyond the turning
of a star,
but in the hearts
of those you left behind
you'll still be part
of everything that's kind and good,
the poetry of life
well-wrapped in wit.
And if from heaven
thou protest
I'll heed you not,
for I have loved you
more than forty years
and know It's true.

MIDNIGHT VISITOR

When the clouds have wrapped around the night,
and trees have caught the stirring of the wind,
across his sleep the dog has smelled the rain,
felt the currents of a summer storm.

Before the human ear has caught the tone
of thunder as it moves around the sky,
he twitches in his dream and starts to moan,
shivers march in furrows down his back.

A cold nose burrows underneath my hand,
two paws are planted firmly on the bed.
Terror's language I can understand,
take the paw and stroke the noble head.

LILIUM TIGRINUM

I have changed my stem.
No longer a delphinium,
orderly in blue,
practical and rather dull,
standing with my cousins side by side.
Who would find my profile
in a crowd?

I'll dress in Tiger Lily clothes.
Arch my neck
and stand alone.
Royalty will want to know my name.
I never thought I'd look so regal,
feel so proud.

WINTER MORNING IN VERMONT

Across our winter view
a curtain dipped in ice
falls down in crystal ribbons
to the ground,
a windowshade of daggers
sheathed in snow.
Between their blades
a patch of clouded sky remains,
how many days
before that too is gone?
Snow dusted mountains
shrink before our eyes,
white pine, birch and fir trees
disappear.
Soon we will be locked within,
while winter plays
her final scene without
this audience of two.

DR. MARGARET HANDY

You sat so often by the side of death,
you knew him well.
Fought to hold
what he would steal away.
Knowledge was your spear,
a smile your gun,
you smothered fear
with laughter where he lay.
Now death has claimed the center of the stage,
the church is full,
the final hymn is sung.
We loved you Margaret Handy, Doctor, friend,
your host of grieving children old and young.

TRIVIA

No time for trivia,
no wish to be tied
by odds and ends.
Details dressed by a restless hand,
lists and notes
on a thin-ruled pad,
cords of words
that you add
with a felt-tipped pen.
Find the scissors
that cut the twine,
dust the spider web with glue.
You polish all the pennies
till they shine.

NIGHTMARE

Sleep throws out his chunky arm
and blinds my eyes,
my forehead crushed beneath his weight
can't turn or twist to either side.
Inert I lie a captive to the schemes
that darkness planned.
I'm lost within a thicket barbed with dreams.

A hostile land where fires rage,
sharp icebergs float with death concealed,
rope bridges sway,
wild animals attack.
At the castle's moat
the bridge is drawn back,
and I am stranded on the other side.

I struggle from the arm of sleep,
throw off his weight
to find what terrors of the day await.
But all is calm,
my covers undisturbed.
Could screams like mine
have really gone unheard?

FOLIE*

Come to my Folie
when heat beats you down,
where the sun on the trees
weaves a fair, golden crown.
I'll whisper of yesterday when we were young,
while you whistle the tune to the songs that we sung.

Come to my Folie
when the noise of the town,
and the voice on the phone
makes your head start to pound.
I'll promise you quietness, hushed and serene,
here in these walls that were built from a dream.

Come to my Folie
when life wears a frown,
and everyone else
is a fool or a clown.
I'll give you my love with its laughter and tears,
come live in my Folie the rest of your years.

* Folie — "A delight" or favorite abode

REEF

Blue-green on black,
the reef hurls back
this angry beauty,
trims its claws
on smooth, wet rock.
High spray is flung
above a tumbled sea,
until it leaves a leaf
of trembling foam,
all frothed and curled.
As wave on wave
sweeps down against the reef
with surging strokes,
the turgid ocean
rushes toward the shore.

THE LECTURER

I'll peel away the flesh
that clothes the bone,
no extra fold will rest
upon its frame.
Expose the nerves
to verbs of flame and air,
catch unaware the spark
that fans the brain
and cut the heated cells
with peels of lime.
You'll hear the clear, terse telegram
I speak,
know every comma binds
your thoughts to mine.
I'll feel your interest soar
beyond yourself,
I've spoken just the proper length
of time.

SHATTERPROOF

Nothing breaks your wall
of calm.
No wrinkles of emotion
seam your face,
yet in a chase for youth
you'd win no prize.
Your eyes hold neither love
nor hate,
they wait for someone else
to feel the pain.
Your empty smile reflects
a hollow man.
You are a fool.

UNCOVERED LIES

Lies are shadows
pasted back to back,
let loose to gallop
through a field of clouds.
But clouds hold rain,
and lies without
their drops of glue
don't sound the same.

THE CENTERPIECE

A talented friend,
full of whimsey and alcohol,
created a centerpiece
in your house,
using one home grown pumpkin,
saltines, peanut butter,
a bed of greens,
and leftovers from the kitchen.
It was smashing.
If I had attempted
such a creation,
being devoid of talent
and usually sober,
you would have smashed my centerpiece
and brought a red poinsettia.

THE VIGIL

You've turned within
yourself,
the focus of your life
is you.
Ill too long to know
or care
that every word you say
is made
of dust and particles of air.
My guilt
at feeling well myself
spellbinds
me to your side,
although
I'd rather hide at home.
Painful days are long,
and nights
grow fungi ripe with fear.
I lean
as near to you as tubes
allow,
and hope I'll die
before
some nightmare of disease
can turn
my tongue into a doped machine.

TOO OLD

I am falling apart.
All my strings are tearing out.
I am a fashion that has passed its time.
The fabric stretched
around a waist that disappeared.

I could live with this.
I never looked for pleasure
in a mirrored wall.
But I remembered every number, face and name.
Who took this gift
has left me maimed
beyond recall.

WORD PICTURE 1910

The houses on the block had awnings,
windows opened to a cool-striped breeze.
Lemonade was served in crystal glasses,
only my mother asked for strong, hot tea.

That day your two great aunts were fighting,
back and forth behind their palm-leaf fans.
I held a parasol to shade my skin
when we went walking down to watch the sea.

AN ARTIST'S VACATION

You paint
in a many-windowed room,
with just the buzzing
of three summer flies
against the glass.
Watching birds outside
who fly with freedom
in their wings.
No need to measure
time in food and sleep,
when eight is always
multiplied by three,
and someone calls the minutes
in between.
Your only mentor
is the canvas and the brush.
So take each hour
by its numeraled toes,
till darkness tickles
on the glass,
then set the easel up
and paint the shadow
of the moon's cold back.

LILACS

You always said to pick the ones I wanted,
to take a lot before they got too old.
I gathered white and every shade of purple,
as many as my outstretched arms could hold.

Every room held whispers of their fragrance,
silver tankards wore a purple plume.
Along with spring comes sadness with the flowers,
you'll never see another lilac bloom.

MEDIEVAL HISTORY

Into a world of words escape,
into a realm where pages reign,
where never one author feels the same
as another.

Into the thoughts of someone else,
curled or straight as a line that ends,
sways or bends till it takes one path
or the other.

Into the lives of Kings and Queens,
never to pass our way again.
Full of rich pageantry and pain —
close to each other.

Into the cellars of History's age,
clocks turn back till the world is young.
Life was cruel but the Minstrels sang
songs to each other.

NO TITLE

Long ago
I gave you my heart,
wrapped in tissue paper,
tied with a slender bow.

You gave it back,
the tissue paper torn,
the ribbon soiled.
It's been so long
since I had to tie a bow.

EPITAPH

If as an epitaph to me
you write,
"She was good at parties,
talked left and right
at dinner,
smiled at bores
and made her hostess laugh,"
I'll surely read the words.

Or if you say,
"She was outspoken
but she didn't lie,
didn't vacillate to please the crowd,
people knew just
where she stood,
but there was room to pass around,"
I'll hear the words.

But if you show
you think of me
by saying nothing to a crowded room,
but miss me
when the lilacs bloom,
when the first fresh snowflakes fall,
I'll know you loved me
best of all.

IN ENVY

One step inside your head,
behind your eyes,
and I would see a world I'd
never seen before.
I'm sure every person
that I met
would wear a different smile
if I were you.
Do colors look the same?
Does spring come earlier to you
in different shades of green?
The sky a deeper blue,
the sun a little warmer
where you stand?
If I could share your tongue
for just a day,
I'd memorize the words
you find to say
that make the other person
wise and full of wit.
Your eyes and ears I'd take on loan,
but if your heart
were ever on display,
I know I'd never give it back.

SNOWMOBILER

Large purple headed beetle,
arms wrapped tight
around the steering wheel,
you steal the quiet
from a winter day.
Across the untracked snow
your monster spits
his acid breath into the air.
He should be made to leave
his spoor on city streets
with others of his gas-filled kind,
while you slide silently on skis
to see the beauty
of a snow-bound world.
Then your fat beer belly
might shrink down beneath your belt.

FOX ENCOUNTER

He was elegant,
a dandy; debonair,
paws placed precisely
on the ground,
muzzle lifted with a rakish air.
He roamed his domain,
field to woods.
Saw me watching,
turned and paused,
black legs poised for instant flight,
he grimaced with a fox-sly stare,
turned his long, luxurious tail
and fled.

TO YOUTH

What right do you have
to swear and shout
and explain to me what the world's about?
If I thought you knew
any better than I,
I'd march along and not ask why.
What makes you think
that you know best,
better than I
who don't protest.
You march to the beat
of a youthful drum,
you are going from where I've come.
If years later
we chance to meet,
on the crowded side
of a distant street,
when age has shackled
your marching feet,
will your band be playing a different beat?

POLITICS

Suddenly I'm out of step.
I never heard the music change.
I used to feel each separate beat,
now hardly recognize the tune.
What game is this we have to play?
I've never had the rules explained,
I didn't know the liar won the prize.
I've read the papers, seen the plays,
listened to the voices, left and right,
yet have still to understand
who told the leader of the band
to change the tune.

VERMONT SPRING

Sing now,
the end of winter
passes through the rings of cold,
on the outer edge of grass
smells spring.

Ice melts,
the streams discover
voices that had slept too long,
slide up and down wet rocks
in song.

Trees grow,
canopies of green
now vaulting roads with awnings
made of colors, sounds and smells
of spring.

TO GOD

I know you dwell
beyond the hills,
above the clouds
and deep beneath the sea.
I've listened to it said
and read in many books
that you are there.
I've heard your voice
when thunder beats the sky,
when waves slap down against the shore.
I've seen how cruel you are to some
who still believe.
I've felt your power
shake the earth,
seen stars ripped loose
to shoot across the night.
I've watched strong men
who pray to you
and cry.
I've heard and seen
and really felt you near,
and yet I'm always asking,
why?

WATER SKIING

Tall weeds
spring up beneath the surface
of the lake,
nod slender heads
as my ski
cuts behind, across
a fast boat's wake,
skims through the water
where their colony is spread.
No clouds
shed shadows
on this clear September day,
no wind
stirs waves
as I ski,
lost in green blue beauty,
island, lake.

NOVEMBER

Gray trees, gray sky,
gray November,
sliding down the outer side of black
to a white December.

Short days, short hours
of faded light,
follow the footsteps of autumn
as the page the bright-garbed knight.

Sad thoughts, sad month
of nature's dying,
brown leaves raked in piles for the flame,
wild geese are south flying.

One day, one year
we met in November,
and started a fire of love
from the spark of an ember.